Being a Happy Mind

SARAH BIZSLEY

The Cloister House Press

Copyright © 2024 Sarah Bizsley

All rights reserved. No part of this publication may be reproduced or transmitted in any form or by any means, electronic or mechanical including photocopying, recording or any information storage or retrieval system, without prior permission in writing from the publishers.

The right of Sarah Bizsley to be identified as the author of this work has been asserted by her in accordance with the Copyright, Designs and Patents Act 1988

First published in the United Kingdom in 2024 by
The Cloister House Press

ISBN 978-1-913460-83-9

Nothing lasts forever –
So, give life a try!

Hello,

I have always been a "book worm" enjoying a lifetime friendship with books. My favourite shop in the world is the bookshop. However, for over a year now, I have formed an intimate relationship with poetry.

Through reading poems every day, I have discovered they have given me the power to help restore and calm my wayward mind, bringing me back to the now. The tangible feeling of poets' words wrapped around my tongue, as if I am appreciating good food or savouring a fine wine, grounds me in the present moment and it feels liberating.

By reading poetry I discovered, unwittingly at first, I was seeing my everyday life through verse. Films I have seen hundreds of times jumped out at me or watching my beautiful children play at peace in their world of imagination and make believe, enabled me to see life through happier eyes. The more I read, the more I wrote.

This is what this is, a collection of happy thoughts I found as I pottered about in my everyday life, and this is something I believe we should all have more of.

As one happy thought a day, the day is one happier place!

So here they are, enjoy!

Sarah

Contents

One Happy Thought   1
   Constant   3
   My Coffee Song   4
   I Like …   5
   Bed   6
   Toothbrush Train   7
   The World is a Symphony   8
   My Girls   9
   My Grandpa   10
   Butterfly of the Mind   11
   The Magic Coffee Pot   12
   See-Saw   13
   I Drink Wine   14
   Glasses of Gratitude   15
   Bookworm   16
   Clifftop Flower   17
   One Happy Thought   18
   The Language of Flowers   19
   Wondering Wardrobe   20
   Pull the Flush   21
   Locating the NOW   22
   As the Waves Roll In   23
   Haiku (1)   24
   Haiku (2)   25
   Haiku (3)   26
   Haiku (4)   27
   Haiku (5)   28
   50/50   29

Good Things	31
Seeds of Happiness	33
A Good Cry!	34
Glorious Sun	35
My Favourite Things:	36
What do they Know?	37
Sounds of the Day	39
Summer Smells	41
The Lady who plays the Piano	42
Painting by Numbers	43
The Toss of a Coin	44
The Imperfect Perfect	45
Memory Lane	46
Inside the Fruit Bowl:	47
An Apple	47
A Pear	48
An Orange	49
A Banana	50
Grapes	51
Clouds	52
Autumn	53
Winter	54
Telltale Signs	55
Sound as a Bell	56
Limericks (1)	57
There was an old man from Bristol	57
There was a young man from Poole	58
There was a young man from Stroud	59
There was an old man from Rayleigh	60
The Lionesses: FIFA Women's World Cup 2023	61

Limericks (2)	62
There was an old lady from Dorset	62
There was an old lady from Swansea	63
There was a young lady from Gloucester	64
There was a young lady from Leicester	65
Talking to Myself	66
Put the Kettle On	67
Worry Balloon	68
For Gerald	69
For Doggy	70
For Bear	71
A Love Poem	72
Proverbially Speaking	73
Lost and Found	74
For I Will Consider	75
Illuminating	76
Moon Magic and Celestial Poem	77
Moon Motion	79
Moonlight	80
Mother Moon	81
Moonstruck	82
Moonbathe	83
Points of View	84
Celestial Bodies	85
Celestial Carers	86
Star Signs	87

One Happy Thought

For Ava, Emily, Alice
My three good things
For Adam
My one happy thought

Constant

The sky is blue.
The grass is green.
The birds sing.
Three good things.

My Coffee Song

Thick. Syrupy. Sweet.
Dark. Strong.
That's how I like it –
My Coffee Song!

I Like ...

I like my morning coffee.
I like my afternoon tea.
I like its warmth and sweetness,
And how I share it with me.

Bed

As my head rests upon its
pillow and I pull the
blanket right up to my chin,
I feel my body unlocking
as its absorbed into the mattress –
I close my eyes and sink in.

Toothbrush Train

Clickety Clickety Clickety Clack
The Toothbrush Train inside of your head
Clickety Clickety Clickety Clack
Used every morning and just before bed.

Clickety Clickety Clickety Clack
Working hard every day and night
Clickety Clickety Clickety Clack
To get your teeth a brilliant bright white.

Clickety Clickety Clickety Clack
Swishing around inside of your mouth
Clickety Clickety Clickety Clack
Remember to say "thank you" as you put it back on the shelf.

The World is a Symphony

The World is a symphony in
perfect harmony sung for you,
sung for me.

Orchestrated through wind chiming trees,
and the sweet, synchronised chorus of bird,
which can be heard, if you:
Stop. Stand still. Listen.

The World is a symphony in
perfect harmony sung for you,
sung for me.

My Girls

The warmth of the sun
The glow of the moon
The wonder in the stars
Are all embodied in you.

I see it in your smile,
I hear it in your laugh,
I feel it by your touch,
An incandescent light Everlast.

The warmth of the sun
The glow of the moon
The wonder in the stars
I discovered them in you.

My Grandpa

Hello Grandpa. I still can see you
with a cup of tea in shaky hands
sitting on your garden bench.

Watching your flowers put on their
show, but it is in you I can see grow
peace and content, as you sit on
your bench.

I can smell your delicious smell of
silk cut tobacco, aftershave, and a
G&T, and with a lopsided smile just
sitting and knowing how to be.

I think, how lucky, I wish I knew
how to be me.

Butterfly of the Mind

Be the butterfly of the mind

Butterflies are beautiful things they
flit through life on grateful wings;
grateful for metamorphosing into
something entirely new; something
fine, through a short passage of time.

Now floating around the sky's blue
dancing from flower to flower,
enjoying each passing hour, and
their newfound freedom of change anew.
Let's learn from these gentle
creatures of kind –

Be the butterfly of the mind.

The Magic Coffee Pot

The Magic Coffee Pot it's a
wonderful thing. Let's lift the
lid and let your heart sing as
aromas fill the nose (inhale deeply).
Taste buds tickling!
Adventure awaits ... here we go!

In the flash of an eye you're
travelling over land, sea and
through sky to the
hemisphere of the south,
where pleasures of the mouth,
can be found through
flavour, texture, and roast;
but which country will boast
their coffee is the best?
Let's visit and put their beans to
the test:
Of Costa Rica, Brazil, and
Peru, but don't forget there's
Kenya too.

But it doesn't really matter
at the end of the day, let's
all lift our hats in praise as
we say "thank you" to the
coffee farmers around the
globe, from which we have
travelled with our nose, as the
magic in coffee will never
stop, it's all here in this little pot.

See-Saw

My name is Anna.
Anna is my name.

I long for summer.
You wait for winter and rain.

The beach, sea, and sand I find my smile.
Mountains, valleys, rocks, hills,
yours takes a while.

I am not sure.
You decide to go.

I say wait.
You say no.

I go up.
You go down.

I want to laugh.
You wear a frown.

I say see.
Saw you say.

I chose my path.
You go your way.

When in conflict with the self,
remember there is always help, to
even the emotional seesaw of the
mind, by being gentle, patient and
kind; and the balance between you
both can be found, is that you are
of the same part and centred at
the heart.

I Drink Wine

I drink wine
Eases my mind
I drink wine.

I drink wine
Frees my mind
I drink wine.

I drink wine
To enjoy time
I drink wine.

I drink wine
To escape time
I drink wine.

I drink wine
As its fine
Vine tastes divine.

I drink wine
To numb fear
I drink wine.

I drink wine
As it's my
Glass of cheer.

I drink wine.
I drink wine.
I drink wine.

Glasses of Gratitude

In the morning when you wake put on your glasses of gratitude and begin the day fresh and anew.

A kaleidoscope of colour bright and light is instantly painted on your eyesight.

You might notice things you didn't perhaps before; clouds jig-sawed throughout the sky played and enjoyed with by birds as they fly.

Trees of all shapes and sizes in their season's finery, striking a pose as they perform their show, standing proud ready to impress, always dressed in their best.

Through your newfound lenses as you wear going about your day here and there, you'll view the world as an enlightened space and that once mislaid smile is back in its rightful place.

When you see life through grateful eyes you'll find, much to your surprise, your mind is at peace and within your reach, happiness floats around on a breeze.

Bookworm

I wish I were a bookworm blanketed
between pages of a book; digesting
each word as I casually look at the
adventures of characters from
which I find their stories, as I
nibble, travel through my mind.

I live in a world of excitement and
intrigue, emotional upheaval as I
read, the words of authors who
have become my friend and thrilled
as ever by the magic of their pen.

What a marvellous way to live a life
from which we can only learn; so,
let's all pick up a book and be like
that wonderful little worm.

Clifftop Flower

Do you know what can be found growing out of a clifftop rock? A dainty, delicate little flower, and within its power, has the ability to shock.

Facing out towards nature's might of pounding waves day and night, thunder, and lightning of raging storms, against aggressive winds it holds its form.

Its will is not eroded, unlike its monolithic nest, it is a flower and growing is what it does best.

Even though the flower may be small, it survives each of nature's brawl, but significantly, remains unphased by it all.

From this we can take great strength in times of trouble when we feel broken or bent, we ourselves have the ability to shock; we are all a little flower growing out of a clifftop rock.

One Happy Thought

One happy thought you believe with
all your heart to be true.

One happy thought in its entirety
belongs to you.

One happy thought like the magical
sprinkling of pink dust, you will
discover is enough, for your arms to
be flung open wide as you feel
yourself soar high into the sky.

One happy thought inside can
ignite a warming glow, a beautiful light.
As it circuits around your body.
overwhelming joy floods your eyesight.

As your eyes are washed clean,
life you will deem, as a friend,
an adventure, a game to play with
again and again.

Believe in who you are, you are a
gift that gives one happy thought a day,
you'll find your greatest
adventure is to live.

The Language of Flowers

There is a universal language everyone can speak. Communicated as a strength for when we feel weak.

In times of happiness, joy and laughter, love celebrating each ever after; and in times of sadness, grief and goodbyes helping us wipe away tears as we cry; the language is given; though no words are said or written; but through a gesture told, silently understood by young and old.

This global dictionary can be found all around us growing out of the ground.

Simply picking a flower, enables you the power, to convey a message without a sound.

When words simply will not do, remember there is always a flower that can say it for you.

Wondering Wardrobe

Every day as I open my
wardrobe I'm presented with an
assortment of clothes.

As I stand and decide what to
wear, arms folded, foot tapping,
naked and bare, I think to
myself, "What do I care?"

Is the day a day to be bold and
brave, back straight ready come
what may.

Or is the day going to be quieter,
simply for me, sitting alone
drinking tea.

Or do I have to be professional,
sensible, and smart lumbered
with the laborious task, of
meeting and greeting skirts and
ties, or can I have an adventure
run off and hide?

Whatever you're doing do not
despair. It doesn't matter what
clothes you wear. As you go
about your day, here and there,
you'll find, every day is a good
day the harder you stare.

Pull the Flush

When you need the toilet do you hold on? No. Because its uncomfortable, it hurts, you want it gone.

So, you go to the bathroom and do what you have to do and instantly feel refreshed from sitting on the loo.

Let me ask you a question. When you have worries and doubts why do you hold on? This is something you shouldn't do; I tell you it's wrong.

Keeping them inside can make you feel just as uncomfortable, in pain, even ill.

When you have worries and doubts, let them out!
Tell a friend, write them down, jump and shout!

When you let them go and they are out of you, you feel as light and as happy as sitting on the loo.

Next time you have worry and doubt, do not hold on. Pull that mental flush, let your worries be gone.

Locating the NOW

If you think of yourself as a pin
and tightly pin yourself down,
stuck without moving, you'll find
you've located the NOW.

Held fast in a precise moment of time and using your
senses you'll discover everything is fine.

What can you see?
What can you hear?
What can you touch?
Breathe: Let go of fear!

When things become too much
and you feel yourself floating
away, pin yourself securely into
your present day.

By doing this simple act and
using your know how, actually in
fact, its yourself you've located
by being in the NOW.

As the Waves Roll In

As the waves roll in pounding
towards me on all four paws, I
feel my body tense a tightening
of the jaw.

Standing on the shore greeted
with a growl and a roar, I brace
myself and close my eyes only to
be met with a pleasant surprise;
of lapping at the feet: cooling,
cleansing, a refreshing treat.

Smiling I look around and see
I'm surround by a mixture of
pebbles, sand, and shingles,
together mingled, under the seas
caressing tongue with each lick
smoothed their rough edges gone.

As I'm kissed by oncoming waves,
realisation slowly dawns, all my
troubles are being washed away.

I feel free, smoothed, anew;
bathed by the ocean's blue.

Feeling alive on the earth's
fringe I stand at peace as the
waves roll in.

Haiku (1)

Misty, fog, and rain
Travelling over the hill –
Suddenly all clear.

Haiku (2)

A magical sight
Blossom on the apple tree:
Spring has sprung.

Haiku (3)

Birds will always sing –
Sun rises after the moon –
And life continues.

Haiku (4)

The evening is dark –
Yet filled with a thousand stars:
There's always a light.

Haiku (5)

Light shining through rain
To help brighten up the day –
Beautiful rainbow.

50/50

Driving towards the cinema I see
you stood with hands in pockets
leaning against the wall.
Nerves quickly turn to panic,
as I realise, you're not alone,
but with all your mates.
Dolled up and feeling rather silly I
assumed it was just us two.
That was our first date.

As I approach you, you apologise,
this was not what you had planned.
It was meant to be just us two as
you lead me by the hand.

From that moment that's exactly
what it was; just us two building
with life's metaphoric blocks.

From the age of sweet sixteen we
have spent each day together as a
team, building from the
foundations laid with block number
one – that evening at the cinema
where our lives begun.

We built a life together equally:
With 50 from you and 50 from me.

Good Things

Thank you,
Grandpa

Seeds of Happiness

Plant seeds of happiness throughout your day and quickly you'll realise your life will feel like the merry month of May.

Let's begin by throwing your seeds up into the sky and watch how they blossom on people passing by.

Such as sharing a smile with someone across the street or being the person who holds open a door for the passing of life's busy feet.

Or as you encounter your daily coffee shop, waiting in line for your favourite brew, look up and meet the person in the eye who made it and say, "thank you!"

As flowers pretty, perfumed, petals cheer and brighten someone's day, these simple little things act in just the same way.

Plant seeds of happiness everywhere you go, then turn, and enjoy the flowers you have sowed.

A Good Cry!

The great, giant, grey clouds –
Like a water balloon poised in the sky –
Ready to burst open for the world to have a good cry.

Eruption! The floods begin!
Washing the earth clean and flushing the air clear –
How clever of Mother Nature to cleanse us with her tears.

A lot can be said for having a good cry,
Letting it all out can make you feel whole.
A chance to start again –
A re-birth for your soul.

Glorious Sun

How glorious it is to sit under the heat of the sun,
And feel your body reacting to its warming light.
Like a flower opening its petals for winter is done:
    Rejoice! Summer is here and all is bright.

My Favourite Things:

Coffee. Coffee. Coffee.
– Happiness in a cup.
Books: the smell of pages, glossy ones are a must.
Stationary of all kinds I relish with childish delight –
Cotton freshly washed all clean and bright.
When it kisses my skin, a great comfort lies within.
My pillow: Soft and cosy – into it I lean, breathing in the smell of me and all my dreams.
The arrival of Spring –
Joy for Winters past.
The anticipation of Summer –
Sunshine at last!
Butterflies flirting through long sunny hours with the pretty petaled dresses of colourful flowers.
My three beautiful girls who opened my eyes to the world; and of course, there's you, who built this life with me –
My friend, my lover: *My Pooey*.

What do they Know?

It is easily argued the rock band Queen is one of the
greatest the worlds ever seen. Captured in blockbuster hits
and Broadway Shows the lives of these 4 stars:
But isn't it ironic to think that Queen's most iconic
Song enjoyed by head banging to in a car,
Was originally laughed at and said that will never happen,
This band will never go far.
Perhaps those "know it all" should have paid better
attention,
and opened their ears to see,
the beautiful masterpiece that is –
Bohemian Rhapsody.

What about Led Zeppelin?
Who most certainly did not go down like a "lead balloon",
But dazzling hard rock and heavy metal as progenitors –
They flew!
One cannot help but wear a smug little grin,
At those who quickly dismissed the mighty Zeppelin.

Let's go further back in time,
To the Impressionist Movement in France.
Which was met with ridicule, insults, and jibes,
But isn't it strange to think it's now
Considered a French national pride?

When you know something is good and you truly believe,
Why listen to the collective critic, what does that achieve?

So, trust yourself because you do know best,
And don't give two figs to the thoughts of the rest.

Go ahead! You know what you can show –
When all they show is what do they know?

Sounds of the Day

Rustling of bedding, a noisy stretch and yawn.
The morning bird is chirping –
A new day has dawned.

With a click of the switch and a splash of the tap –
(As you swish your mouthwash and spit your toothpaste),
Then hear the roar of the shower as it blasts hot water in your face.

Opening chest of drawers, closing wardrobe doors.
Deciding on the days clothes as you pace across creaking floors.

Toast popping and the singing kettle waiting to fill your favourite vessel, with coffee or tea and as you jingle your keys, take a quick slurp, now it's time to leave.

Joggers running on the street the: Thump! Thump! Thump!
Of their pounding feet.

Car horns beeping, bus brakes screeching, engines ticking over for no one can get through –
The traffic jam is endless, radios blaring a tune to entertain us, as we wait all stuck in this que.

Above all the ear bashing mayhem, like a constant gong –
Your ears prick to something beautiful – Birdsong!

The clickety tap, tap, of computers, tablets, and phones,
buzzing and beeping of notifications reminding you to roam,
app after app, as you tap this and tap that.

The humdrum chorus of the coffee shop –
chatter, chatter, chatter it never stops.
Steaming of milk, grinding of beans all encapsulated by
the great coffee machine.

Shopping: Waiting in another que at the till, bombarded by
announcements of which offers can reduce your bill.
The dull whine of a squeaky trolley wheel, driving you
slightly insane as you were choosing tonight's meal.

Home: As you open your front door you can feel your ears smile.
Deafening silence is most welcome – it's been a while!

As you flop on the settee, making yourself comfy,
an eruption of noise startles you, as you turn on the T.V.
A growl in your stomach you no longer can ignore. It's
time to get up and commence the evening chore –
Of cooking dinner as you partake in the kitchen band –
Drumming along with all your pots and pans.

Rustling of bedding, but before you switch of the light,
Your ears hear your voice say:
"Thank you for my day – Goodnight!"

Summer Smells

Freshly cut grass and the warm perfumed air –
Of petals bathed in sunlight.
Swimming pools and chlorine-soaked hair.

The scent of suncream on hot bronzed skin.
The mouth-watering smell of a BBQ.
The tickly sensation of fizzes up the nose from the refreshment of fruity ciders: Sipped, savoured, enjoyed all summer through.

Each of these a memory my nostrils know so well –
I love how the summer smells.

The Lady who plays the Piano

Captured by the rawness of feeling she can hardly contain.
If you look into her face, you can see she's in pain.
But, before her heart breaks, she knows it's time to flush her emotional IV line.

As she sits at the piano, but before she plays, gently caresses each key so the piano knows just what to say.

As her fingers dance along its entirety –
All she feels is downloaded into her sweet melody.

As she finishes a small smile appears –
All that torments inside has been erased – disappeared!

Standing quietly behind her I understand my emotions better as they flow –

As I listen to the lovely lady who plays the piano.

Painting by Numbers

Painting by numbers – if you think about it, it's a totally bizarre thing. To be told how a masterpiece should look by somebody you've never seen.

Painting by numbers this concept is now rife in our everyday life.
Everywhere you turn there's instructions on how to look, behave, and be, and we listen – but why should we?

Aren't we all different, baring blank canvases, to explore creativity and our own uniqueness?

As famously once said:
"To thine own self be true."
So, if you want to paint by numbers, remember, the numbers should be chosen by you.

The Toss of a Coin

When faced with a difficult decision, and you don't know what to do. You feel like you're going round in circles, tormenting yourself for how do you choose?

Do I turn left?

                                                          Do I turn right?

I know, I'll let a coin decide.

But the thing about flipping a coin is, everyone's got a favourite side.
When you throw your coin up into the air, you know which way you want it to land –
Therefore, the answers lie with you, they haven't been taken out of your hand.
When it comes down to the toss of a coin, remember, you have a preferred side.
So, when facing a difficult decision, trust your instincts and you'll be fine.

The Imperfect Perfect

From graceful swans gliding effortlessly over a lake, but if you look underneath there's frantic, erratic, movement of legs too frightened to take a break.

To the blushing bride in all her majesty –
But I wonder how long it took, for her this way to look, complied out of tears, stress, and anxiety?

Or the famous composer of operatic genius to the masterpieces hanging on gallery walls –
Again, I wonder how much of these were constructed out of tempestuous temper tantrums, and petulant brawls?

Why do we bother with perfection when really there is no such thing? It bears no real substance, it is a glossy coating, a pretty sheen.

**So, it seems to me, to end up as considered perfect –
You first must be the perfect version of imperfect.**

Memory Lane

As you grow older you will find you've been laying slabs as the hands of time, have been silently ticking the days away, whilst you've been busy cataloguing your life down on memory lane.

With every paving stone, slab, and pebble laid, each contains a memory made. It doesn't matter what they hold (be that of young or be that of old), they are a part of you and a tale to be told.

Sometimes, without warning you may trip, on the upturned corner of a flagstone's lip. As you stumble into your younger self, feeling disconcerted, searching around for help – Stop!
Remember this simple truth – all you are doing is falling into you.

Embrace each memory both bad and good, they've equally paved the way to where you are now stood.

Try to welcome and treat both the same –
as you turn and look down memory lane.

Inside the Fruit Bowl:

An Apple

Shiny, crisp, refreshingly sweet:
The crunch of its offering between your teeth.
Brightly coloured, picked from its tree –
As a delicious treat for you and me.

A Pear

The happy bell inside the Fruit Bowl:
With gentle curves, feels nice to hold.
Its grainy, sweet flesh, which is so fair –
Is a delight on your tongue, that pretty, pale, pear.

An Orange

Sitting at the centre like the radiant sun:
While other fruit orbit its orange sphere one by one.
As you peel back its glowing skin –
Its sunlight bursts open for you to drink in.

A Banana

Lying on its side staying very still,
It hugs each fruit and within its will,
Of a caring, kind, nurturing embrace –
Ripens its fellow friends at a quicker pace.

Grapes

Jaunty, jolly, juicy, gems:
Who play hide and seek amongst fruity friends,
Inside the Fruit Bowl. As you try to find
One, it slips through your fingers – every time!

Clouds

Clouds like sponges soaking up sunlight.
Blanketing the world from its sunshine.
How wonderful to see a hint of blue sky –
   As the clouds break and pass by.

Autumn

Adjusting to the colder weather as –
Umber colours are painted everywhere.
Time to seek out all your warmer clothes –
Underwear: thick, woolly, knitted –
Made to keep you comfy, cosy, and warm –
Now Autumn is here.

Winter

Nature suddenly stopped – Paused in time!
Just until the sun remembers again how to shine.
No life. No growth. A darkened light.
Its silence is deafening and oh, how its chill bites.

Telltale Signs

Look what's that? The daffs are out!
The first sign of Spring!
To lazing in summer grasses, weaving daisies into chains,
And being oh, so jolly!
Hang on a sec! Now the kids are acting bonkers,
playing with little brown conkers –
Autumns on the wing!
Suddenly with force winter arrives,
But how merry with its pretty sprigs of holly.

Sound as a Bell

If you feel like you have bitten off more than you can chew and you've lost your smile to a frown – life is getting you down, Pause. Please don't fall, under the weather, because there is something you can do, however, hard it may seem; let me spill the beans and you will know what I mean ...

Take a moment to yourself and speak like a friend. Have that mental rest, away from stress, just until you clear your head, and then, with your best foot forward, you can continue instead.

Remember the ball is in your court, and the long and short, it is your life so, come rain or shine, you have the power to be fine, through acts of self-love and care, realise the person who is always there is: I, YOU, and ME – Be nice to that person and you will succeed!

Do something different –
Change your view, pull a rabbit out of a hat and on seeing that –
There is nothing you cannot do.

Basically, in a nutshell, wear a smile and you'll be
Sound as a Bell!

Limericks (1)

There was an old man from Bristol:

There was an old man from Bristol.
When walking was pricked by a thistle.
With a yelp and a howl –
Skilfully hooted like an owl –
That tuneful old man from Bristol.

There was a young man from Poole:

There was a young man from Poole.
Whose dog loved to drool.
No matter the shoe –
They were always soaked through –
That poor young man from Poole.

There was a young man from Stroud:

There was a young man from Stroud.
Who was regarded as awfully proud.
With his head held high –
He nearly touches the sky –
That austere young man from Stroud.

There was an old man from Rayleigh:

There was an old man from Rayleigh.
Who loved golf and played it daily.
He was never glum –
When scoring a hole in one –
That sporty old man from Rayleigh.

The Lionesses:

FIFA Women's World Cup 2023

11 individual players standing on a pitch.
Transformed into one by the iconic stitch –
Of a badge bearing three Lions sewn onto a shirt,
Synchronised, worn, through blood, sweat, and dirt.

Now this single player moves with a forceful grace,
holding its own with every challenge faced.
And is personified at the start of play in:
Carter, Greenwood, Bright finding a way –
To the might of Daley, James, and Bronze –
Onto the power houses of Russo, Hemp, Toone and beyond.

But this Lion's Heart does not finish lying on its feet, but continues to beat, with Earp's Golden Glove proudly raised even in defeat.

Thank you to every girl who rushes outside to kick a ball with national pride. For this simple truth you are not alone, for who you inspired you brought it home.

So, here's to the Lionesses no matter the score –
Let's give it up for the girls and hear them **ROAR!**

Limericks (2)

There was an old lady from Dorset:

There was an old lady from Dorset.
Who made bridal corsets.
She was never down,
When making a gown –
That happy old lady from Dorset.

There was an old lady from Swansea:

There was an old lady from Swansea.
Who looked after a bumblebee.
Wherever she goes,
It sits on her nose –
That kind old lady from Swansea.

There was a young lady from Gloucester:

There was a young lady from Gloucester.
Whose pet was a red lobster.
She named it Bob,
Didn't care people thought it odd –
That crazy young lady from Gloucester.

There was a young lady from Leicester:

There was a young lady from Leicester.
Who loved whizzing around on her Vespa.
In the flash of an eye,
She quickly scoots by –
That nippy young lady from Leicester.

Talking to Myself

Sitting as an older woman with a cup of tea clasped in hands,
My mind travels down the vista of years to all my dreams and plans –
That I never had the courage to follow, make happen, or come true,
And I realise the only person I've failed is the one sitting here – is you.

If I could go back in time and speak to my younger self,
I would say: "*Listen! Sod the thoughts of everybody else.*
Trust what makes you happy. Believe in what you're good at.
Following your dreams is right. So, hold your own, be brave,
And don't give up the fight."

Back to sipping my tea and as the penny drops –
I realise I'm alive and kicking I haven't stopped.
All those dreams, plans, and desires, are still inside me –
So now is the time to start creating and realise I ***still*** can be...

Yes, my yesteryear may have been and gone –
But my future is present, let's begin, come on!

Put the Kettle On

(For Sophie)

Suzy put the kettle on to make a cup of tea –
To listen to my broken heart, so I'll feel less lonely.

Katy put the kettle on to make a cup of tea –
To share her insecurities about having another baby.

Sophie put the kettle on to make a cup of tea –
To offload the stress on her chest, by having a good rant and rave.

I put the kettle on to make a cup of tea –
To put the pieces of my life together, and finally become brave.

We all put the kettle on to make cups of tea to celebrate the joys of life, and to find comfort in those long goodbyes.

A problem is never a problem for long –
When you go and put the kettle on!

Worry Balloon

Here's a worry balloon. Shall I show you what to do?
First pick a colour, mine's yellow which will you choose?
Let's begin! By slowing blowing it up
With all your worries from each little puff.

It's almost full, keep going, don't stop!
Now stand back and watch your worries go POP!

For Gerald

I love seeing you sit, your gangly limbs all over the place.
With one leg jauntily thrown over the other, brings a smile
to my face.
You look so funny; I cannot help but laugh –
I guess it's true what they say:
You're having a Giraffe!

For Doggy

I remember when we took a trip to the farm,
And there he was – it was love at first sight!
You scooped him up and held him under your arm,
And he's been with you since then every day and night.

He may be old, tattered, and rough –
But he is well worn from all your love.

For Bear

Hello Bear! Can I have a word?
I just want to say thank you for all the love you give to her.
You make her happy, a special friend she
takes everywhere –
I'm so glad I saw you on the shelf just sitting there.
Now you sit under her love and care –
This sweet, blessed, little brown bear.

A Love Poem

Your imaginative, crazy, steadfast mind helps you shine
when you create, and you create when you shine.
You tickle me pink with your idiosyncratic ways, similar to
the flamboyance of a panto dame.
Your nurturing touch is felt – sublime!
And I am made special being seen through your eyes.
I call you perpetual sunshine for that is what you are.
A bold bright light, fixed like the stars.
Each day you see joyfully through the azure of your eyes –
happily sanguine.
This strength you have amazes me and you carry it in
bundles, heaps, and reams.
A beautiful, sweet creature who has a gently soul –
The love I have for you bounds me together – whole!
You are kind and warming, with a fairy like grace,
flittering your magic which can be traced, by the smiles
you leave all over the place.

The peace I have inside me, comes from loving all of you
three.
Every day with you seeing through your eyes the world –

**What a fine, happy place it is, because of three
beautiful girls.**

Proverbially Speaking

From generations to generations the good old folk have got it right. Passing down their general truths and pithy sound advice. On how to pull your socks up and make the most out of this beautiful life.

So, make hay while the sun shines and strike while the iron is hot. As the early bird catches the worm so keep going do not stop.

Sometimes though you will find a change is as good as a rest, but do not put the cart in front of the horse or let the grass grow under your feet, as a journey of a thousand miles begins with a single step, so hold your own, walk your path, and don't give way to defeat.

It does not matter if you fall down, what matters is you stand back up, as it is no use crying over spilt milk, just grab another cup.

Always try your best and keep your head held high and mind, fine words butter no parsnips, is a word said to the wise.

Keep planting those walnut and pears for your heirs and enjoy your life and times, don't forget a problem shared is a problem halved, and a stitch in time saves nine.

And remember one more thing –
A cat can look at a king.

Lost and Found

Not all who wander are lost as the saying goes.
But what about those who are amidst life's throes –
What can we do to locate spiritual serenity and find a place within us we can call home?

If you can't see the wood for the trees, how do you navigate around? By shunning your inner compass to leap and bound,
Towards your common go-to as a quick fix to feel safe and sound?

Avast this behaviour as it will never do, to find yourself you are free to choose the guidance of your magnetic north and trust the direction it paves, its course.

Go forth, take comfort under your feet is solid ground –
As to be lost means you can be found.

For I Will Consider

For I will consider at the age of 38 I still haven't got the foggiest about life.
I am still trying to find my feet, to figure myself out –
What it is I am meant to do, and poignantly, like who I am, whilst trusting the path my feet are walking on at the same time.
For this I will perform in ten degrees:
Firstly, I've noticed things of joy are usually found when you are not looking for them.
Secondly, when you are not thinking so much – when your mind is free from fog, peace settles.
Thirdly, if I trust to keep going – putting one foot in front of the other I know I'll arrive in the end.
Fourthly, I might encounter beautiful, unexpected delights along the way.
Fifthly, I might bump into a strength I forgot I had to heal old wounds.
Sixthly, if I remember to look up, I might smile.
Seventhly, to keep walking my path I might meet a friend.
Eighthly, I might notice that friend has been with me all along.
Ninthly, my friend is my path.
Tenthly, my path is me.
For I will consider happiness is the path, I am my path –
Look Up!

Illuminating

To stand under the Godly Sun when you find yourself in a tizz –
Pulls you up short to how wonderful life is.

Moon Magic

And Celestial Poems

For
Every Moonchild

Moon Motion

The wax and wane of our inner tidal emotions,
Rise and fall with the cyclical Moon Motion.

Moonlight

In the midst of night,
She rises setting the mood.
Her mesmerising, mediative light,
Calms, quiets your subconscious mind –
The magical, melatonin moon.

Mother Moon

Her gentle, rhythmic movements ease the tides of sleep.
And with her alluring melodic tunes,
Lullabies us into slumber –
Our nurturing Mother Moon.

Moonstruck

You have affected the workings of my mind,
no rational or logical thought.
I feel completely unearthed – a crazed lovesick loon!
Now suspended in a dream like state –
whilst anxious and thwart,
For I have been struck by the ethereal moon.

Moonbathe

Alone walking at night, I see,
You have been waiting patiently.
As I approach, your face exposes all of me –
I am now open and free.

Being bathed by her lustrous beams,
I become purified from her deep celestial clean.

Standing strong. Balanced. Belong.
In a powerful state of tranquillity –
My moment: Moon and Me!

My holistic healing is complete I am saved –
As I stand alone and moonbathe.

Points of View

Astrologers and Astronomers both look up into the skies,
In their quest to find the answers to the unattainable
question – Why?

Both observe the movements, motions,
of celestial bodies up above –
Whilst divided on their points of view –
They unite only on this:
To ascertain how we came to be here,
our understanding of life,
and what is true.

Celestial Bodies

The celestial bodies of the sun, moon, and stars,
    We choose to parent us from afar.

Their offerings to energise, nurture, and guide,
Help us find peace and make sense of the time we spend alive.

Celestial Carers

The fierce father figure burning in the sky,
Along with the calming, nurturing, Mother Moon,
Together, equally, protect their offspring – Earth:
And energise, vitalise, control rhythmically the ebb and
flow of the child's inner rising tides for its life to bloom.

Star Signs

For millennia we have looked up to the skies,
for answers, guides,
directing our journey along the path called life.

Trusting the fixed points of light,
twinkling above us throughout the night,
to navigate our body, mind, and soul,
– these astronomical objects –
we religiously map in order to feel whole.

But I wonder if these celestial charts,
Are written in the stars,
As a pathway to our salvation which starts,
When you follow the gaze of your destined stars?

Or arguably is it true to say,
The celestial bodies of night and day,
We pin our hopes onto for us to understand,
Why we are here, is there a universal plan?

Or like the sun, moon, and stars,
Which we admire from afar –
Do we simply exist orbiting each other,
As rogue planets that sometimes jar,
For we are all just tiny wandering stars?

It is a wonder, to wonder on the stars.
Their light emanates a beacon of hope for us all.
Our fascination, desire,
to reach the unattainable still thrives,
As we are children of the cosmos after all.

To my best humans ever
(you know who you are)
Thank you for believing in me.

Milton Keynes UK
Ingram Content Group UK Ltd.
UKHW010614250624
444652UK00001B/37